A Journey Through
Northumberland

Clive Crossley – Graeme Peacock

Preface by the Duchess of Northumberland

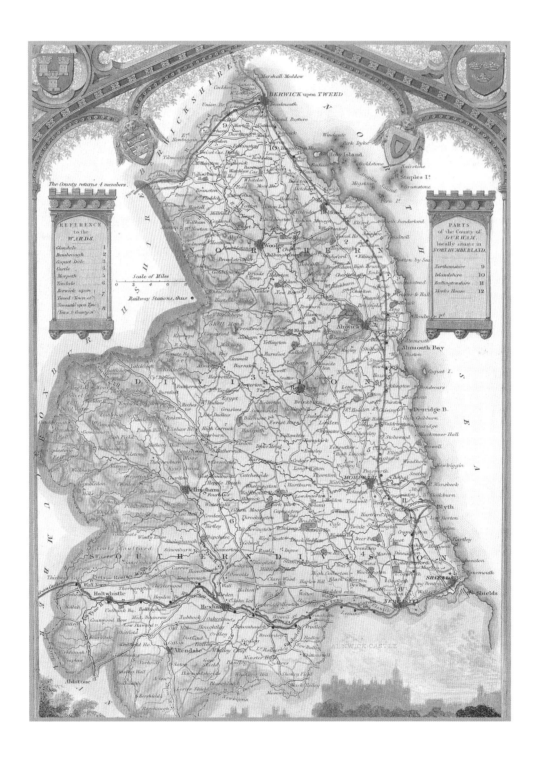

Map of Northumberland c1847 Moule

With the exception of the boundary changes in 1974 which resulted
in the separation of Newcastle and North Tyneside,
Northumberland has largely retained its historic form

CONTENTS

Preface   4

Foreword   5

Introduction   7

Chapter 1   Forming the Landscape   9
             The forces which created the landforms of Northumberland

Chapter 2   Establishing a Presence   29
             The first human settlement in Northumberland – the achievements
             of prehistoric people – Roman power and influence – the departure
             of the Legions

Chapter 3   The Golden Age   49
             The establishment of the kingdoms and culture of the Anglo-Saxons –
             the coming of Christianity – the visitation of the Vikings

Chapter 4   A Lawless Border   71
             The Norman subjugation – bloody border warfare – the building of
             castles and defences – feuding, raiding and lawlessness – the Union
             of the Crowns

Chapter 5   Taming the Landscape   99
             The coming of peace – the triumphs of trade and agriculture –
             the creation of stately homes and gardens – the hardships
             of the new agricultural workers

Chapter 6   Revolutions in Steam   125
             The growth of manufacturing – domination by coal – formation of the
             railways – industrial achievement and human suffering

Chapter 7   A New Identity   149
             The decline of deep mining and heavy industry – crises in employment
             and communities – repairing the environment – changes in the towns
             and countryside – investing in a new future.

Index   172

Further reading   174

Appreciation and image acknowledgements   175

It is a great pleasure to contribute to this new guide which captures the history of Northumberland in words and images. This is a County which is rich in memories and traditions, a County in which heritage has not been consigned to centres and museums but is here in the open to be encountered at every turn.

The achievements of Capability Brown and the great Northumberland landscape gardeners inspired our work in creating The Alnwick Garden. This book will I hope stimulate others to explore the history of the land and people of Northumberland and find similar inspiration.

Jane Northumberland

The Duchess of Northumberland

FOREWORD

I am extremely pleased to welcome you to this fine new guide to the County of Northumberland. Through text and photographs we aim to introduce you to the long history of Northumberland and to show how its present identity was created.

The story is a remarkable one. The volcanic eruptions which formed our highest hills were a prelude to a human history in which strife and achievement would be joint themes.

This was a frontier land and armies and raiding parties raged across our County over many centuries. Defensive features, such as Hadrian's Wall and our many imposing castles, still dominate the landscape and provide a constant reminder of a past in which conflict was commonplace.

Northumberland has also been distinguished by remarkable achievements. The preparation of the magnificent Lindisfarne Gospels, the development of intricately landscaped parklands, pioneering work in mining and railway engineering, the establishment of England's largest reservoir and Europe's largest man made forest, all are associated with this County.

The constant background to this turbulent and eventful history are the varied and special landscapes of Northumberland. Through the photographs and illustrations in this book we aim to capture the qualities of the hills, the lowlands, the valleys, the coast, the towns and the villages of Northumberland. This is a setting worthy of a stirring story. I am proud to invite you to explore the County of Northumberland.

Councillor Michael Davey

1st Edition 2003
Published by Northumberland County Council
Designed and produced by NB GROUP
Copyright©Northumberland County Council

This book offers a glimpse into the 420 million years of landscape evolution and the 8000 years of human history which have created contemporary Northumberland. The story begins with the formation of the land mass which was to become Northumberland and through several chapters traces the main actions and events which successive generations played out in this landscape. Northumberland is a county within which history is everywhere evident. It is a county within which our countryside and towns have largely retained their traditional character. These enduring qualities invite the use of photography to unfold the story of this County. Throughout this book, liberal use has therefore been made of images both new and old.

In a short book there is inevitably much which must be omitted and further exploration of the physical landscape of the County and the many excellent published works on its history are both recommended. The focus of this book is on events within the present boundaries of the County. It must not be forgotten however that at stages in its history, Northumberland was a centre of power and influence which extended way beyond the Tweed and the Tyne. From strongholds in Northumberland the military and political might of the Northumbrian Anglo-Saxon kings and great landowners such as the Dukes of Northumberland was felt in many parts of the British mainland. From cultural and religious centres such as Lindisfarne Christian influences spread throughout Britain and into the European mainland.

In looking at the main themes in each period of the history of Northumberland, some important events and developments are given limited attention. Whilst for example the best known castles and fortifications are associated with the long period of border conflict, the construction of defences has continued into more recent times. Although it has not been possible to describe their development in the thematic chapters of the book, a visit to many of the County's long sandy beaches will nevertheless reveal the crumbling concrete of pill boxes and tank traps designed to hinder invasion during the second world war.

It is, however, the little recorded stories of the ordinary men and women who formed the armies and worked on the land and in the industries of Northumberland which underpin this story. In old field patterns, in the earthworks of deserted villages, in the hulls of abandoned boats and in the remains of old mines and industries, some glimpses may be gained into these lives. It is hoped that this book will encourage exploration of the County, of the buildings and places for which it is well known and of little discovered features and landscapes which also speak of a unique history.

Forming the Landscape

Coquetdale

Northumberland has a character that is quite distinct from any other English county. Although renowned for the open spaces and dramatic, sweeping views within its coast and countryside, Northumberland also has landscapes where towns and industry dominate. It is a county where within a few miles gentle parkland changes to high heather moor, where Iron Age hillforts overlook modern day forests and ordered farms surround warlike castles. That Northumberland today is a county of contrasts is, in part, a consequence of a long and turbulent human history. Although this dramatic story is the subject of this book, the creation of the landforms of Northumberland is associated with time scales and forces which dwarf the history and strivings of humankind.

The earliest evidence of the formation of Northumberland is given by the shales and sandstones found in places close to the Scottish border. These date back about 450 million years to a period of earth history known as the Silurian when this area was deep ocean. At this time the area destined to become Northumberland lay far south of the equator and was being squeezed between two continents. The vast stresses resulting from these earth movements crumpled and folded the rocks deep in the earth's crust. The rounded, grass covered slopes of the Cheviot Hills are the remains of a huge volcanic complex which formed as a result of these stresses and

then erupted vast quantities of lava and ash around 400 million years ago. Outcrops of grey baked lava at the Bizzle and Hen Hole are visible reminders of these dramatic times. In contrast, brightly coloured agate pebbles are to be found only by those prepared to search in the cold waters of Cheviot steams. These agates were formed in steam holes in the lava into which mineral rich waters seeped and eventually formed as rock. Towards the close of the period of volcanic convulsions, moulten rock which did not reach the surface solidified as granite which today forms the Cheviot itself.

Eventually, about 350 million years ago, more tranquil conditions were established as the future Northumberland subsided beneath a wide tropical sea. This marked the beginning of the Carboniferous period. By now our area lay almost astride the equator, the continent having drifted northwards. Lime-rich sediments which accumulated on the floor of this tropical sea, are preserved today as beds of limestone which can be seen exposed on parts of the coast, for example around Beadnell, inland in mid Northumberland and locally in the Roman Wall country. Fossils of corals and shells within the limestone give a clue to the wealth of life in environments similar to the present day seas off the Bahamas.

Above left: Pebble of Cheviot agate
Above right: Synclinal fold in the Great Limestone with shale layer above, Mootlaw Quarry

For much of the early Carboniferous period, however, rivers draining land masses to the north and north-east were bringing vast amounts of mud and sand into the sea, periodically building great deltas and converting large parts of our area into low lying tropical swamps. We see these muds and sands today as shales and sandstones. On occasions, exceptionally large and powerful rivers crossed these deltas, depositing huge amounts of sand in their channels. The Fell Sandstone of the Simonside Hills and the sandstones of Shaftoe and Rothley Crags are amongst the rocks which have been formed from this deposition. The delta surfaces were repeatedly colonised by lush forests of primitive trees and ferns which, as they decayed and were covered by later deposits of mud and sand, formed into coal seams. Such coal-forming swamps developed on many occasions in the Carboniferous period, but became especially common during later Carboniferous times when the group of rocks, known from their abundance of coal seams as the Coal Measures, were laid down. It is from these rocks in the Northumberland Coalfield that millions of tons of coal were won over many centuries. Between the coal seams, the sand deposits were compressed into sandstones which have themselves been extensively quarried. The character of the County's architecture owes much to the use of local sandstones, many of which have been widely used as important building stones elsewhere in Britain.

During roughly 60 million years of the Carboniferous period, layer upon layer of sedimentary rocks, in places in central Northumberland several kilometres thick, accumulated. Earth movements, beginning in late Carboniferous times, gently folded and tilted these rocks towards the east and south. These movements were accompanied by the stretching and cracking of the rocks, causing vast quantities of molten rock, or magma, to rise from deep within the earth's crust. Unlike the molten rock which erupted to form the Cheviot volcanoes, this late Carboniferous magma never reached the surface but was injected, about 295 million years ago, between the layers of sedimentary rock, rather like the filling in a sandwich. Where weaknesses existed in the layers of sedimentary rock, the magma squeezed upwards forming vertical dykes. As the magma cooled, it crystallised, forming the hard black rock known as dolerite. This group of intrusions is one of Northumberland's most celebrated geological features, known as the Great Whin Sill. The sill underlies much of eastern and southern Northumberland and extends southwards into the Pennines and County Durham.

Disused sandstone quarry and remains of crane, Ford

Erosion of the Carboniferous rocks and Whin Sill over millions of years has given rise to some of Northumberland's most distinctive scenery. A protective cap of coarse Fell Sandstone has resulted in the long curve of heather clad hills which are such a characteristic feature of central Northumberland. Standing clear from the surrounding lowlands, where softer shales have offered less resistance to erosion, the Kyloe Hills, the Chillingham Ridge, the Doddington Moors and the Harbottle and Simonside Hills are prominent in the landscape. In the south of the County

the deposition of successive series of sandstones, limestones, shales and thin coal measures has resulted in the distinctive high moorlands of the North Pennines into which have been cut the deep valleys of the Allendales and South Tyne. It is the outcrops of the Whin Sill that have resulted in perhaps the most dramatic landscape features. This hard and extremely resistant rock forms the Farne Islands, the rock upon which Holy Island Castle stands, the cliffs at Bamburgh and Dunstanburgh and, perhaps most notably, the dramatic central section of Hadrian's Wall.

Soon after the intrusion of the Whin Sill, warm mineral-rich waters deep within the earth began to circulate in cracks and faults beneath the Pennines and Tyne valley. As they cooled they deposited minerals, including galena, the main ore of lead which was mined for centuries in the south of the County. Associated with lead were traces of silver and an abundance of other, so-called 'spar' minerals such as fluorspar, barytes and witherite, all of which have been worked as industrial raw materials.

In the last major phase in the creation of the landforms of Northumberland, beginning about 2.5 million years ago, it was forces of cold rather than heat which were to dominate. As a result of widespread global cooling, ice sheets covered the County during several phases. This ice scoured the existing landscape, left huge deposits of boulder clay, gravel and sand upon it and moved massive rocks. Much of the south and east of the County is overlaid by great thicknesses of these glacial deposits which can be clearly seen today as exposures of boulder clay in the coastal cliffs. The rapid increase in temperature which marked the end of the last Ice Age, about 10,000 years ago, brought about a rise in sea levels that drowned vast areas of land which once would have continued the surface area of Northumberland far to the east. It is probable that the invasion of the sea drove early peoples inland. Here they were to discover territory which was being colonised by forests and was becoming a fit place for human habitation. The eventful human history of Northumberland was about to begin.

Above: Dramatic colours revealed when grey Whin Sill dolerite viewed through a microscope
Right: Outcrops of hard andesite lavas at Braydon Crags in the Cheviot Hills

Fell Sandstone eroded by the River Coquet at Thrum Mill, near Rothbury

15

Fell Sandstone boulder, scoured and moved by ice, the Drake Stone,
Harbottle Hills

Hotbank Crags. Exposures of the Whin Sill along Hadrian's Wall

Bamburgh Castle. Sited on an exposure of the Whin Sill

Linhope Spout. Resistant portions of Cheviot Granite and intrusive rocks
within it give rise to this striking waterfall

Top: Simonside Hills. Exposures of Fell Sandstones

Above: Weak Carboniferous rocks with thick overlay of glacial deposits forming
a flat plain for the River Till. In the background are the volcanic landforms
of the Cheviot Hills

Top: Piper's Chair, Shaftoe Crags.
Sandstone boulder supported by weaker strata

Above: East Allen Valley, near Allenheads.
Deep cut North Pennines valley with surrounding high moorlands

Top: Belsay Quarry, the source of building stone for Belsay Hall

Above: Belsay Hall

Coal Measures laid bare. Stobswood opencast coal mine

Gentle forces of erosion, an upland stream

24

Carboniferous rock exposed in the sand, Alnmouth Bay

Hen Hole, Cheviot Hills. A corrie formed by the powerful erosive forces of ice

Whinstone cliffs, Dunstanburgh Castle

Resistant whinstone columns providing protected nesting sites, Farne Islands

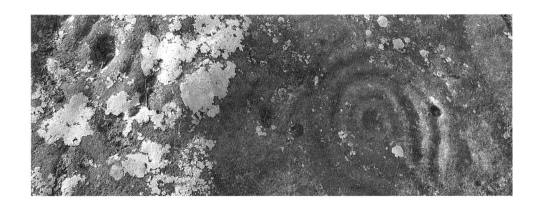

Establishing
a Presence

Prehistoric rock art, Roughting Linn, near Ford

We cannot be sure about the date of the first human presence in what is now Northumberland. It is probable, though, that small groups of people first began to explore the landscape following the melting of the northern ice sheets and the establishment of Britain as an island. From about 6000 BC onwards, considerable numbers of Mesolithic people were gaining a living through hunting

and fishing. Scatters of flints produced by these people in the making of tools have been found throughout the coastal plain in locations such as Newbiggin-by-the-Sea and Budle Bay. At Howick, near Craster, the recent discovery of the foundations of a Mesolithic house offers evidence of early settlement near the coast.

It was during the Neolithic period (about 4000 to 2500 BC) and the Bronze Age (about 2000 to 800 BC) that the human impact on the Northumberland landscape became significant. As agriculture began to develop and settlements were established people began to build ritual monuments and permanent places for the dead to rest. In the Milfield Plain, below the Cheviot Hills, standing stones and henges (circular enclosures associated with rituals and ceremonies) were erected, features which still remain buried beneath fields to this day. Recent archaeological excavations in the Milfield Plain have indeed revealed a henge enclosing over a hectare of land. Care was also taken in the burial of the dead. Many hillsides throughout Northumberland display distinctive mounds which conceal Bronze Age burial remains. At Lordenshaws, above Rothbury, there is particularly clear evidence of such burials with stone-lined burial cists (coffins) widely scattered amongst the heather. Erosion on the coast has also revealed burial sites and a cist which was recently exposed is displayed within Druridge Bay Country Park.

The most enigmatic remains from the late Neolithic and Bronze Age periods are the rock carvings, collectively known as cup-and-ring markings, which can be found throughout Northumberland on outcrops of the Fell Sandstones. Particularly fine examples are at Lordenshaws, Roughting Linn near Ford, and on Doddington Moor.

The significance of these detailed carvings has long been forgotten, but it seems possible that they conveyed messages about tribal boundaries, identified important route ways or, more tantalisingly, represented aspects of spiritual beliefs.

Above left: Mesolithic flints found at Budle Bay
Above right: Bronze Age flint arrowhead from Rothbury

Evidence of the beginning of the long history of human conflict in Northumberland is to be found towards the end of the Bronze Age. With an expanding population

and a marked deterioration in the climate, demands on the reducing amount of fertile land would have become intense. Settlements which had previously comprised scattered, unenclosed farmsteads were now more closely packed together and defended by wooden stockades. Increased demands for wood and the need to expand agricultural land to support a growing population would have hastened the process of clearing the native forests in Northumberland.

The Iron Age (about 800 BC to AD 40) saw the building of wooden stockades superseded by the construction of more massive hillforts on many upland vantage points. Multiple ditches and high ramparts of earth and stone defended the most elaborate of these structures. Fine examples of hillforts may be seen at Brough Law in the Breamish Valley, at Ros Castle above Chillingham Park and at Old Bewick near Eglingham. The most impressive hillfort, in terms of scale, caps the domed hill of Yeavering Bell near Kirknewton. Enclosing an area of seven hectares, this hillfort contains the remains of 130 circular family huts and was probably a major tribal capital. In the later Iron Age it seems that peace and stability may once again have become the norm and this is reflected in the expansion of settlements and field systems outside defended sites.

It was in this landscape which already had a long human history that the Romans established their military presence around AD 80. First developing forts and bases at Corbridge and Vindolanda and along the east-west supply route of the Stanegate, the Roman army under Agricola then marched northwards building Dere Street as

a supply route and constructing further forts on its course, at High Rochester and at Chew Green on the Cheviot Ridge. To the east of Dere Street a further route north was developed, a road, the purpose of which became forgotten during the passing centuries, acquiring the name of the Devil's Causeway.

Above left: Gold hair ring from Alnwick, late Bronze Age
Above right: Inscription from Milecastle 38, Hadrian's Wall

Towards the end of the first century AD the Romans withdrew from Scotland and the Stanegate between Newcastle and Carlisle became the new frontier. Inspecting his territories soon after his accession as Emperor in AD 117, Hadrian visited Britain. Considering the existing fortifications along the Stanegate inadequate as the northern frontier he ordered that work begin on the creation of a barrier which would 'separate the Romans from the barbarians'. Now a World Heritage Site, Hadrian's Wall and its associated features comprise the most impressive surviving monument in Europe to the military power and organisational genius of the Roman Empire. The Wall was to extend 76 miles from the lowest crossing point of the River Tyne in Newcastle to the shores of the Solway at Bowness in Cumbria. As originally planned, the Wall was to be 10 Roman feet wide (2.9 m), around 15 ft high (4.6 m) and to have the additional defensive strength of a 'V' shaped ditch to the north, 26 ft (8 m) in width and 10 ft (3 m) in depth. At every Roman mile a milecastle was constructed which combined the functions of a gateway through the Wall and a fortlet to defend it. Such was the desire to implement imperial dictates to the letter that milecastles were located at specified distances even where that resulted in building taking place on an apparently unsuitable site. At Cawfields, for example, the milecastle is sited uncomfortably on sloping ground and has been built to include the regulation gateways even though the steep whinstone crags make through access virtually impossible. Equally spaced between the milecastles were two turrets which served as observation towers. In Northumberland the Wall was built of stone and faced with a thick weatherproof coating of lime mortar. Finished in this way the Wall would have appeared as a startlingly white barrier sweeping across the landscape and making a dramatic statement of Roman power.

Carved stone head of Antenociticus, Hadrian's Wall

Over the period of nearly 300 years during which the Wall remained operational, many modifications were introduced. At an early stage it was decided to incorporate the main forts which housed the garrison troops within the Wall itself. These forts and their associated vicus (civilian settlements) provided for the military and domestic needs of the Roman garrisons. The remains of the fort sites at Vindolanda, Housesteads and Chesters are accessible today and offer a fascinating insight into life on the Wall. A further major design change was the construction of the Vallum, a broad flat-bottomed ditch with flanking banks, located on the south side of the Wall. Although occasionally breached, the Wall continued to provide the main element of the Roman defences until the recall of the Legions early in the fifth century. To appreciate the awe-inspiring scale of Hadrian's Wall as an undertaking of military engineering it should, if possible, be viewed on foot. In particular, explore those sections within the Northumberland National Park where the Wall rises high on black whinstone crags and commands all the surrounding landscape.

Whilst the Wall provides the greatest attraction and interest to visitors it is the Roman roads in Northumberland and in particular Dere Street which provide the continuing link between the imperial world and our own. Originally constructed by Agricola to service and supply his invasion into Scotland, the route of Dere Street north from Corbridge can be followed along the present A68 road and then as a green track as it rises up to the wild countryside of the Cheviot Ridge and the exposed marching camps at Chew Green.

With the ending of the Roman occupation a period of two centuries ensued for which we have few written records of life in Northumberland. This time of apparent instability was, however, to be the foundation for an age when Northumberland became the base of a new military power and a centre for a cultural and spiritual awakening.

Above left: River God Tyne, Roman carving in stone found at Chesters
Above right: Aemilia finger ring, Roman, found at Corbridge

Bronze Age burial cist, Lordenshaws, near Rothbury

Poind and His Man. Prehistoric burial mound near Bolam.
During the long period of border lawlessness, nightly watches were set
on this prominent location to warn of Scottish raids

Prehistoric rock carvings, Roughting Linn, near Ford

Stone circle near Duddo

Prehistoric rock carvings, Lordenshaws, near Rothbury

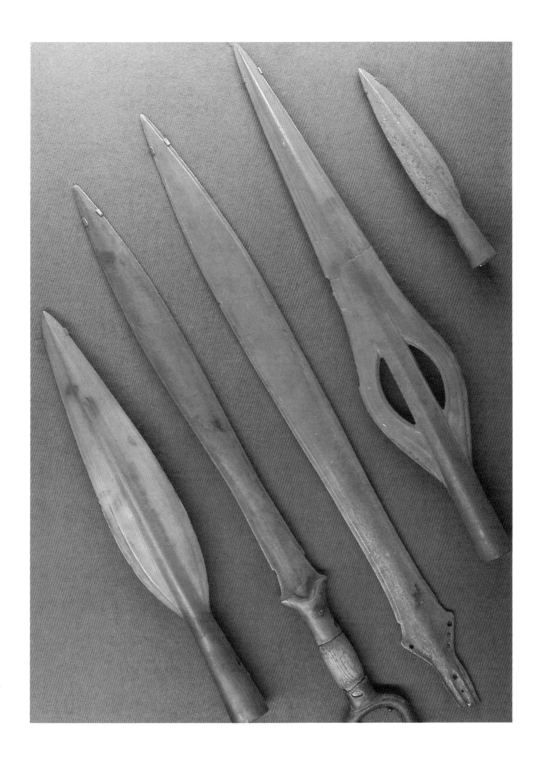

Bronze Age swords and spears found near Whittingham

Yeavering Bell hillfort, near Kirknewton

Brough Law hillfort, Breamish Valley

Chesters Roman Fort (Cilurnum) guarding a bridging point over the North Tyne

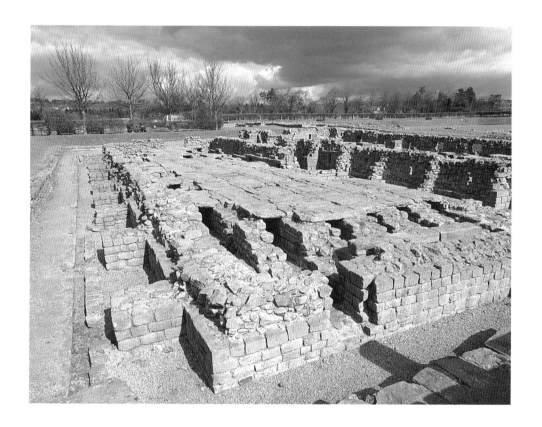

Granary buildings within the Roman fort at Corbridge

Milecastle 42, Cawfields. The location of this milecastle, according to
the specified plan for Hadrian's Wall, has resulted in its north gate
being sited above vertical cliffs

Top: Hadrian's Wall, following the high whinstone crags and descending
towards Housesteads Fort

Above: Vindolanda Roman Fort and the straight route of the Stanegate

Aerial view of Chew Green. Remains of a Roman fortlet on the left
and a temporary marching camp to the right

Excavations in progress on a Bronze Age burial cairn at Turf Knowe, Ingram. This low mound of stones was found to contain several 4000 year old cremations, some of which were held within attractive pottery vessels

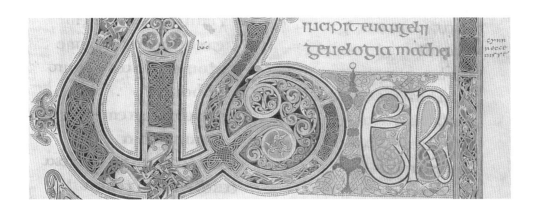

THE GOLDEN AGE

Initial page of Gospel of St Matthew, Lindisfarne Gospels (f27)

The Roman army in Britannia was recalled to protect the imperial provinces in mainland Europe during the early years of the fifth century, as constant attacks by armies of Germanic warriors threatened the integrity of the empire. As the structures of the empire began to crumble, those troops who remained in northern England were often unpaid and little was done to maintain the defences of the Wall. Soldiers eventually turned to farming and other civilian occupations to maintain themselves and their families and the now abandoned Wall began a long and undignified history as a source of building stone. Into the new power vacuum were to surge invaders. Picts from the Scottish Highlands and Scots, whose origins lay in Ireland, were amongst the peoples moving out from their homelands seeking territory, plunder and power. However, the settlers who were to have the most marked impact on Northumberland, were to cross the sea from the north European mainland. By the sixth century peoples of Germanic origin were the most numerous element of the population in this part of the country. The foundation was in place for the development of the great Anglo-Saxon Kingdom of Northumbria.

By the mid-sixth century two ruling Anglo-Saxon kingdoms controlled the north of England, Bernicia to the north of the River Tees and Deira to the south. Under the kings of Bernicia (Ida and his grandson Æthelfrith), campaigns of aggressive expansion were launched. Æthelfrith conquered the competing kingdoms of Strathclyde to the north, Rheged to the west and Deira to the south. Edwin, the vanquished King of Deira, formed an alliance against Æthelfrith, killing him in battle and forcing his sons Oswald and Oswiu into exile on the island of Iona. Edwin rapidly expanded his influence and territories, developing a network of alliances and leading his army to conquests in Wessex and North Wales. Bamburgh (on the Northumberland coast) was a main military base for this expanding kingdom and at Yeavering, near the foot of the Cheviot Hills, a royal palace complex was constructed complete with a spectacular 'grandstand' for gatherings of the people. To cement one of his many alliances, Edwin married Æthelburh, the daughter of Eadbald of Kent, the first Christian king in Anglo-Saxon England. As part of Æthelburh's marriage contract she was allowed to bring a Christian mission to Northumbria under the Italian bishop, Paulinus. The mission proved a remarkable success, with Edwin and all his nobility converting to Christianity at York in 627. Baptisms followed throughout Northumbria, with one ceremony at Yeavering lasting a total of 36 days. Edwin died in battle in 633 but his conqueror, King Cadwalla of Gwynedd, the 'Black Prince of Wales', was himself defeated soon after by Oswald the exiled son of Æthelfrith at the battle of Heavenfield near Hexham.

Although Oswald's reign was to last only eight years, it was to result in Northumbria being confirmed as the dominant kingdom in the land, with conquests and alliances extending its power and influence into eastern and southern England. Oswald was also renowned during his lifetime for his devout Christianity and works of charity. Following his death in battle on the Welsh border, parts of his severed body were taken to the churches at Lindisfarne and Bamburgh which then became associated with acts of miraculous healing.

Determined to establish a firmly based Christian kingdom in Northumbria, Oswald had been instrumental in bringing an Irish monk named Aidan from Iona to Holy Island. Aidan travelled on foot throughout Northumbria preaching, baptising and aiding the poor and the dispossessed. The piety of his life was such that he was credited with numerous healing miracles and particles of wood from the post upon which he was leaning at his death were reputed to have remarkable curative powers.

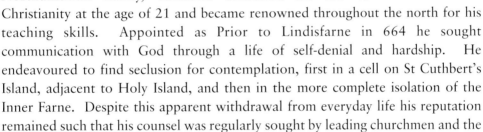

The inspiration of Aidan was to direct the life of Cuthbert, Northumbria's most famous saint. Born into a noble Northumbrian family, Cuthbert dedicated his life to Christianity at the age of 21 and became renowned throughout the north for his teaching skills. Appointed as Prior to Lindisfarne in 664 he sought communication with God through a life of self-denial and hardship. He endeavoured to find seclusion for contemplation, first in a cell on St Cuthbert's Island, adjacent to Holy Island, and then in the more complete isolation of the Inner Farne. Despite this apparent withdrawal from everyday life his reputation remained such that his counsel was regularly sought by leading churchmen and the king and queen themselves. On his death, Cuthbert's body was transported back to Lindisfarne where his grave by the altar at the Priory Church became an object of pilgrimage. It was, however, the alleged discovery of his uncorrupted corpse, when his grave was opened eleven years after his death, which confirmed his veneration and ensured a lasting fame.

It is thought that the discovery of St Cuthbert's body, in a seemingly miraculous state of preservation, may have been the inspiration which led to the production of the sumptuously decorated Lindisfarne Gospels. Symbolising the flowering of Anglo-Saxon culture, during a period which became known as the Golden Age of Northumbria, the Lindisfarne Gospels reveal Mediterranean and Celtic influences as well as native artistic traditions. The repeated use of bird decorations in the manuscript appears to reflect the particular influence of Lindisfarne which was then, as now, a haven for a multitude of seabirds.

Above right: Anglo-Saxon hanging bowl from Capheaton
Above left: Anglo-Saxon cross shaft from Alnmouth

Intricately carved stones dating from the Golden Age are a further remarkable artistic inheritance and again show the fusing of several cultural traditions in Northumbria. Although the Anglo-Saxons had never been known to carve in stone before, the coming of Christianity proved the inspiration for the creation of stone art of the highest quality. The carved high cross decorated with Christian imagery is the most striking product of this work. The Rothbury Cross shaft, which now forms the base of the font at Rothbury church, the head of the Rothbury Cross and the remains of the Alnmouth Cross and Nunnykirk Cross, which are all displayed in the Museum of Antiquities in Newcastle upon Tyne, are amongst the finest of these works which still remain.

Although there are now few standing remains in Northumberland, the Golden Age was also a period which was remarkable for the building of churches and monasteries. The leading figure in this building programme was Wilfrid, a member of the Northumbrian aristocracy who studied at the monastic church at Lindisfarne. The building project for which he is best known in Northumberland was the church at Hexham, built on the site of the present day abbey. Whilst there are few features now remaining above ground of the impressive basilican-style church which Wilfrid constructed on this site, the mysterious underground crypt, within which precious church relics would have been housed, may still be seen. However, the most notable contribution of Wilfrid to the Christian history of the nation was his advocacy of the doctrines of the Roman church over the competing teachings of the Irish church. Following the triumph of Wilfrid's arguments at the Synod of Whitby in 664, it was the Roman orthodoxy, with its greater emphasis on ceremonies and ecclesiastical hierarchies which was to be the dominant doctrine in Northumbria and in the nation until the time of the Reformation.

Whilst King Oswald and many of his successors were to die in battle, Northumbria remained a large and powerful realm until late into the eighth century. Constant feuding between claimants to the throne at this time was, however, to severely undermine the power of the Northumbrian kings. The weakened kingdom was to be dealt a series of devastating blows from new invaders from the east, the Vikings.

One of the first Viking raids on England fell on Lindisfarne in 793. Here the rich treasures of the monastery would have offered a tempting target to the invaders. Over the succeeding decades, the Vikings made ever deeper incursions into England and finally, in 876, the Anglo-Saxon Chronicle records that their leaders 'shared out the lands of the Northumbrians'. In the face of continuing raids the monks on Lindisfarne were compelled to flee, taking with them their most sacred treasures. The body of St Cuthbert was itself removed and reputedly hidden in remote locations such as the overhanging outcrop of sandstone rock near Holburn, now known as St Cuthbert's Cave.

To the Anglo-Saxon churchmen of Northumbria it seemed that these destructive raids by an irresistible foreign power and the resultant changing order of society heralded the imminent end of the world. A gravemarker on Lindisfarne, dating from this period, depicts conquering Viking warriors on one side and the Day of Judgement on the reverse. The Golden Age of Northumbria had been brought to a close.

Right: Modern statue of St Aidan, Holy Island

Artist's reconstruction of the royal Anglo-Saxon centre at Yeavering
in the early 7th century

Church of St Oswald, Heavenfield. Built to commemorate the victory of
King Oswald over the pagan King Cadwalla

Statue of St Aidan, Holy Island

Holy Island

Illustration from the Gospel of St John, Lindisfarne Gospels (f209v)

Carpet page preceding the Gospel of St Luke, Lindisfarne Gospels (f138v)

St Cuthbert's Island, off Holy Island.
Once a retreat for Northumberland's most famous Saint

Gold and garnet pendant cross of St Cuthbert

The crypt built by Wilfrid at Hexham Abbey

Late 7th century bishop's throne from Wilfrid's church
at Hexham Abbey

Anglo-Saxon artistic influences have continued through to the modern age

Top: St Cuthbert's Church, Inner Farne. On the supposed site of St Cuthbert's cell

Above: St Cuthbert's Cave, near Holburn, an alleged resting place for the
coffin of the Saint on its long journey from Lindisfarne

Cross on the site of the former Anglo-Saxon church at Church Hill, Alnmouth

St Mary, Holy Island. Located immediately to the west of the Priory,
this church has features which suggest a Saxon origin

Gravemarker from Lindisfarne, with band of Viking warriors on one side
and a representation of the Day of Judgement on the other

Right: Holy Island

A LAWLESS BORDER

Warkworth Castle

The Norse Vikings were to control the north of England until the 10th century when the wave of recovery by native rulers, which began with the victories of King Alfred in Wessex, swept into Northumbria. Northumbria now became an earldom situated uncomfortably between the heartland of the English realm to the south and the Scottish kingdom to the west and north. Warfare with Scotland was to flare and it was indeed an early Scottish victory at the battle of Carham in 1018 which was to tentatively fix the border on the River Tweed. A long period was beginning during which conflict and instability were to become the normal currencies of life.

It was from the south of England, however, that the forces came which brought an end to the remnants of the ancient kingdom of Northumbria and led to the creation of the County of Northumberland. Achieving victory at Hastings in 1066, William the Conqueror was to direct his energies to subduing first the south of the country and then, more terribly, the north. The brutal suppression of an early revolt in the north led to Yorkshire, the southern part of the earldom of Northumbria, coming directly under William's rule. Imposing a new earl who had scant regard for Northumbrian opinions, William triggered an uprising which led to the murder of his appointee. Taking revenge, in his customary manner, William ordered the ravaging of Northumbria under Odo of Bayeux. A final revolt by Earl Robert of Northumbria in 1095 brought about swift suppression and direct rule by William II under an appointed sheriff, with local control by twenty one barons. Although some areas of land around Norham, Holy Island and Bedlington were placed under the control of the Bishop of Durham and were collectively known as North Durham, the County of Northumberland had effectively been born. The creation

of Northumberland did not, however, determine whether the County should be an English or Scottish possession. For eighteen years during the early 12th century Northumberland was indeed ruled by successive heirs to the Scottish throne. It was not until 1237 that the Scottish claim to Northumberland was formally abandoned. In that year the Scottish king Alexander II met with the English king Henry III at York and brought about a permanent legal settlement by relinquishing his family's claim to the Earldom of Northumbria.

Tosson Tower near Rothbury. The rubble remains of a 14th century tower house

Although conflict was the dominant theme of the Norman period it is important not to overlook some lasting, non-military achievements. The programme of ecclesiastical building was particularly remarkable. The ruins of Lindisfarne Priory on Holy Island, Hulne Priory near Alnwick, the finely preserved monastic churches at Hexham and Brinkburn and the form of the abbey and village at Blanchland provide impressive memorials to the spiritual beliefs of the age. Whilst few remains are evident of the 12th century nunnery at Holystone, originally founded by the Benedictines, the secluded Lady's Well near the site retains a unique atmosphere of calm and contemplation. The early 11th century through to the 13th century was a period of extensive building and remodelling of Northumberland's parish churches. Major parts of impressive churches, such as St Laurence at Warkworth and St Andrew at Corbridge, date from this time. The Norman period in Northumberland has  also left an inheritance of churches, including St Aidan at Thockrington and St John the Baptist at Edlingham, which are made distinctive by their unassuming simplicity.

The main landowning families in Northumberland retained their Norman passion for hunting and undertook the large scale enclosure of land to create deer parks. These provided the attraction of predictable success in the hunt and a ready supply of fresh meat. Particularly fine examples of deer parks are Hulne Park at Alnwick which once extended to 5000 acres (2000 ha) and Chillingham Park, which also enclosed and protected the famous herd of wild cattle. The traditions of the deer park influenced the development of landscaped parkland and managed upland grouse moors in later, more settled times.

The abandonment of the Scottish claim to Northumberland did not, as may have been hoped, mark the end of conflicts between England and Scotland. Edward I, 'the hammer of the Scots', began his long and violent campaign to subjugate the Scottish nation at Norham Castle in Northumberland. Here, in 1291 and in Berwick-upon-Tweed, the following year, he adjudicated between claimants to the Scottish throne, finally deciding on the weak and seemingly compliant John Balliol. Balliol though was persuaded by his barons to make an alliance with France against England, and this gave the pretext for Edward to launch his first invasion across the border in 1296. The bloody conquest of the then Scottish town of Berwick-upon-Tweed was his first military act and – in a pattern which would be repeated over the centuries – the Scots responded with savage raids into Northumberland. Recognising the critical strategic importance of Berwick, Edward directed the building of massive stone walls around the burnt and devastated town.

Above left: St Aidan, Thockrington
Above right: St John the Baptist, Edlingham

Three centuries of conflict were to ensue after Edward I first led his army across the Tweed. During this time, Northumberland, as a border county, withstood numerous ravages from opposing armies. It was Robert the Bruce who, in his defiance of the claim of the English crown for fiefdom over Scotland, wrought the greatest misery on Northumberland. Defeat of the English army under Edward II at the battle of Bannockburn left Northumberland exposed to the wrath of the Scottish forces. The devastation of war, accompanied by poor harvests, was such that the tithes collected by the churches at Norham and Holy Island declined from their normal levels of about £400 per annum to average less than £20 in the years 1317 to 1321. Even in the south of the County rents from Ponteland village declined from a peacetime level of £34 per annum to only £4 in 1325.

With the death of Robert the Bruce and the accession of Edward III to the English throne the balance of power was to reverse and crushing defeats were inflicted on the Scots at Halidon Hill near Berwick-upon-Tweed and at Neville's Cross near Durham. The cycle of war again changed after the death of Edward III, with the Scottish army raiding as far south as Newcastle and proving victorious against a force led by Sir Henry Percy (Hotspur) at the battle of Otterburn. Hotspur was to take his revenge following a second Scottish raid on Newcastle by securing a decisive victory at the battle of Humbleton Hill. As competing forces ranged across the County the suffering of the people of Northumberland was great. In one terrifying raid by the Scottish king, William the Lion, the village of Warkworth was laid waste and 300 of its inhabitants burned to death within the village church.

Conflict brought riches to some, as well as hardship to many. Services to the Crown through battle were to lead to the rise of several families, most notably the Percys, who by 1400 became the dominant landowners and possessors of the earldom of Northumberland.

To reinforce the network of royal and baronial castles at Bamburgh, Norham, Alnwick, Harbottle, Mitford, Morpeth, Prudhoe, Wark-on-Tweed, Wark-on-Tyne and Warkworth, new castles were built during this period at Dunstanburgh, Bothal, Chillingham, Ford and Ogle. Fortified lesser castles or hall houses were built by Northumberland Barons. These varied from intricate structures such as Aydon Castle to more basic fortifications like that at Edlingham. More numerous, still, were the fortified towers built by the second rank of landowners in the County. Over one hundred of these impressive structures were constructed by the early 16th century. In the strategically located settlement of Elsdon, the high and solidly formed Elsdon Tower is one of the finest of those that remain. The clergy themselves saw spiritual protection was insufficient in these troubled times and at Ford and at Corbridge the structures of vicars peles or towers, still survive.

Elsdon Tower

Occasional damaging incursions into Northumberland by Scottish armies were to occur through the 15th century. The last major set piece battle in the County was

in 1513 when, taking advantage of war between England and France, the Scottish king, James IV, came over the border with a massive force thought to have numbered over 30,000 men. After successfully capturing Norham, Wark, Etal and Ford castles the Scottish army was eventually brought to battle at Flodden Hill near Branxton. Exposed to artillery fire, James IV led his pike wielding infantry in a fateful charge down the hillside, during which he and a large part of his army fell beneath the swinging blades of the English bills. Although conflict between England and Scotland continued throughout the 16th century the trauma of Flodden appears to have been such that no further major battle between the Scottish and English crowns was to be fought on Northumberland soil.

However, fear of an invasion by the Scots, supported by their French allies, remained ever present and major programmes of reconstruction were undertaken to bolster the border defences. The castle at Wark-on-Tweed, one of the most important and fought over strongholds on the border, was rebuilt following its capture and part destruction by James IV before Flodden. A new keep was constructed, four storeys high and, by contemporary account, 'in every stage, there is five grete murdour holes (canon ports) shut with grete volutes of stone... so that great bumbardes may be shot out....' Around this massive keep, a ring wall was constructed 23 ft (7 m) high and 6 ft (1.8 m) thick, with platforms for artillery.

Whilst at Wark-on-Tweed extensive works have been required in recent years to conserve the last crumbling remains of the once imposing castle structures, at Berwick-upon-Tweed, the massive Elizabethan defensive walls remain in a remarkable condition. A town of great strategic importance, Berwick had changed hands ten times between Scotland and England as armies had repeatedly breached its defences. Inspired by ideas from Italy, deeply reinforced walls were constructed during the reign of Elizabeth I, their mutually supporting arrow head bastions providing what was seen to be the ultimate defence against the cannon and men of an invading army. The walls, the most expensive single project undertaken during the Elizabethan reign, were never tested by war, but now offer one of the most dramatic short walks in Northumberland.

Above left: Harbottle Castle, once a key part of the border defences
Above right: Mitford Castle

The last decades of the 16th century were to be a time of frightening lawlessness throughout the borders. A breakdown in formal systems of defence and of obligations between landowners and tenants caused some border areas to revert to near banditry. These problems were particularly endemic in the Tynedale and Redesdale areas of Northumberland. Here family clans, including the Charltons, Dodds, Halls, Hedleys, Milburns, Reeds and Robsons, engaged in blackmail, stealing animals and kidnapping (collectively known as 'reiving') as a major part of their livelihood. The objects of their raids were other family clans, often from across the border but sometimes neighbours, who returned their aggression in equal measure. Although the reivers were often a key part of English and Scottish armies their allegiances were principally to family and their motives family gain. At Flodden the reivers performed a crucial role in securing victory for the English but then plundered the baggage and stole the horses of their erstwhile compatriots. Scottish borderers undertook a successful charge early in the battle then stood aside to observe the outcome and returned at night to pillage the dead.

Securing the conviction of miscreants proved extremely difficult, with the government-appointed custodians, the Wardens of the Marches, having insufficient money and men and facing the widespread intimidation of witnesses. The confession of 'Geordie' Burn, a reiver facing a relatively rare conviction, offers some insight into the brutality of their lives. "He voluntarily of himself said that

hee had lived long enough to do so many villanies as hee had done; and withal told us, that he had layne with about 40 men's wives, what in England what in Scotland, and that hee had killed seven Englishmen with his own hands, cruelly murdering them; that he had spent his whole time in whoreing, drinking, stealing, and taking deep revenge for slight offences." Hexham Gaol was to have a role in bringing apprehended reivers closer to final justice and now contains a museum which records their misdeeds.

With the failure of Government to enforce the law, the people in the dales and surrounding districts had to improvise ways to protect themselves and their possessions. A common response was the building of small fortified farmhouses or 'bastles'. The bastles were squat, thick-walled defensive buildings, comprising a protected ground floor room into which stock could be herded in the evenings or when danger threatened and a room above for the family, access to which would be by a retractable ladder or protected staircase.

Above left: Woodhouses Bastle, near Holystone
Above right: Hexham Gaol

Lawlessness in the borders was gradually brought under control as a result of determined action by James I after the Union of the Crowns in 1603. The legacy of this period of terror may still be seen in the dales and valleys in the south-west of the County, where the often crumbling remains of bastle houses are a still common feature. The restored bastles at Woodhouses, near Holystone and at Black Middens, on the edge of Kielder Forest allow appreciation of how life would have been during this period of constant danger.

The history of armed conflict with Scotland was not, however, brought to a final conclusion with the Union of the Crowns. Scotland became an active participant in the English Civil War and in 1644 sent a large army southwards through Northumberland in support of the parliamentary cause. The nobility and gentry of Northumberland had considerable representation in the ill-fated Jacobite rebellion of 1715 with several losing their lives and having family estates confiscated as a result. The role of Dorothy Forster in rescuing her brother, Thomas, from execution, by having him smuggled out of Newgate Prison, is established in popular legend. The second Jacobite rebellion of 1745 and the invasion into England of a Scottish army led by Bonnie Prince Charlie caused a renewal of concern about the state of defences and military infrastructure in Northumberland. The construction of the military road (now the B6318) between Newcastle and Carlisle and the building of the impressive barracks in Berwick-upon-Tweed were

major projects which resulted from this fear of future unrest. Northumberland was to have a decisive role in the final suppression of the warlike Highland clans who were the shock force of the Scottish armies. After centuries of warfare and countless thousands of deaths, the critical occupation of the Highlands and the displacement and pacification of the clans was achieved by the humble Cheviot sheep.

Above left: Berwick Old Bridge, built following the Union of the Crowns in 1603
Above right: Berwick Barracks, constructed in 1717 in response to the first Jacobite uprising,
these were the first purpose built barracks to be built in Britain

Chillingham Castle. Hunting the wild cattle within the Norman deer park

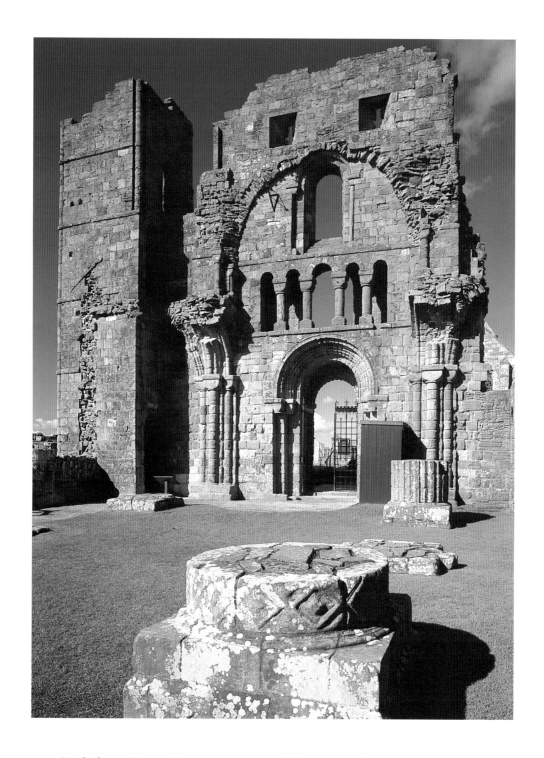

Lindisfarne Priory. Picturesque ruins of the Priory Church, originally built
by the Bishop of Durham in the early 11th century

Hexham Abbey. With the original church founded by St Wilfrid destroyed during
the period of the Viking raids, the magnificent 'Abbey' was founded in the
12th century as the church for an Augustinian priory

Right: Brinkburn Priory. Finely restored in 1858, this medieval Augustinian priory
church is located in beautiful seclusion within a loop of the Coquet river

Blanchland Abbey. The church of St Mary the Virgin built by the
Lord Crewe Trustees around the remains of the old monastic church

Lady's Well, Holystone

St Laurence, Warkworth. A fine Norman church

Bamburgh Castle

Preston Tower. A 14th century hall tower with the addition
of a 19th century clock

Right: Alnwick Castle. An ancient castle site on which successive generations
of the Percy family have built and rebuilt

The White Wall, Berwick-upon-Tweed. Remains of the medieval town wall

Norham Castle. The chief northern stronghold of the bishops of Durham
and a mainstay of the border defences

Artist's reconstruction of Wark-on-Tweed Castle

Warkworth Castle from the River Coquet. Probably built by Henry, the son of
David I, king of Scotland when he became Earl of Northumberland, the Castle was
extensively rebuilt under the Percy family and was for many years their principal
base in defending against Scottish raids

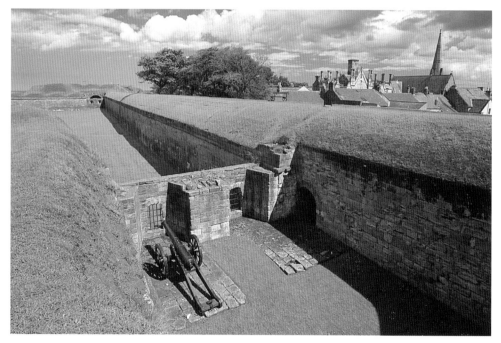

Top: Berwick Quay Walls

Above: Berwick Walls leading to Brass Bastion, massive Elizabethan defences,
designed to resist artillery attack

Memorial on the site of the battle of Flodden

Vicar's Pele, Corbridge. Built of Roman stone, this medieval tower house
provided protection for the clergy

Prudhoe Castle. A strong defensible site above the River Tyne

Holy Island Castle. A Tudor fort built to defend the strategically important
harbour at Holy Island. In the foreground are the remains of staiths
for ships taking lime from the island

Top: Edlingham Castle, near Alnwick. A manor house with complex fortifications
Above: Aydon Castle. A fortified hall strategically sited above the Cor Burn

Taming
THE Landscape

Wallington Hall

The stability which resulted from the cessation of border conflict was to provide the foundation for a period during which the County was subject to profound forces for change. The key to change was the introduction of new agricultural practices and these in turn stimulated developments which were to transform both the appearance of Northumberland and the ways of life of its people.

The ever-present dangers of border life before the Union of the Crowns in 1603 and the need to maintain a base of manpower for defence hindered the processes of change in rural life which were being introduced in other parts of England. The fact that the ownership of land in Northumberland was concentrated in the hands of a few individuals enabled the change, when it came, to proceed at an unprecedented speed. In 1604 the Border Survey initiated by James I noted of Redesdale 'certain high lands called summer grounds are used as summer or sheiling grounds by the whole inhabitants of the Manor, wherein each man knoweth his sheiling stead; and they sheild together by Surnames; not keeping Cattle according to the proportion of the rent, but eating all in Common without

stint or number'. It was the replacement of such ancient practices by the enclosure of land and by the introduction of contemporary and efficient agricultural systems which resulted in the farmed landscape we see today. In turn, it was the wealth created by this new agriculture and by trade and industry which was to lead to the development of the stately houses and surrounding gardens and parkland which now form an integral part of the rural landscape.

The valleys and plains of Northumberland contain much land which is extremely fertile. Given peace, expanding markets for their produce and knowledge of new systems of agriculture, the major landowners in these areas were ideally placed

to transform their estates into efficient and prosperous enterprises. Throughout the lowland areas of Northumberland new field systems were created with thousands of miles of hawthorn hedges. Landlords and farmers, such as Horace St Paul and the Culley brothers, introduced new agricultural management systems and practices which by 1800 had established a national reputation for Northumberland as a County of agricultural innovation.

Above left: Ploughing the land, an engraving by Thomas Bewick
Above right: Abandoned lime kiln

Old settlements which did not fit into models of efficient agriculture were levelled and new farmsteads established. These new farmsteads, constructed on the principles of the urban factories of the day, remain as distinctive features in the rural landscape. Frequently these farmsteads still display the circular or polygonal horse gins and the chimneys for steam engines which would once have powered threshing machines. Adjacent to the farmsteads, rows of small cottages which originally housed the workforce of farm labourers still remain a common feature. With most of the naturally fertile land in full production landowners turned their attention to the higher moor lands. Here, through enclosure, drainage and the application of copious amounts of lime, valuable agricultural land was created from that which was previously considered waste. Today, the overgrown remains of small quarries and squat stone-built lime kilns mark this period when the moors were tamed.

Stability and increasing prosperity was the background for the first major road building programme in Northumberland since Roman times. It was, however, the concerns which preoccupied a previous age that led to the construction of the first of the major new roads. The Jacobite rebellion of 1745 had resulted in a Scottish army, led by Bonnie Prince Charlie, invading England and reaching as far south as Derby. The poor condition of existing roads had hindered the interception of the Scottish army and as previously noted, a direct response was the building of the military road between Newcastle and Carlisle. In an act of destruction which no modern day motorway building project could rival, the foundation for much of this road in Northumberland was provided by Hadrian's Wall. Between the mid-18th and the early 19th century, commercial rather than military benefits were the stimulus for a major programme of road improvements. This period witnessed the formation of 19 turnpike trusts and the development of soundly constructed highways which form the basis of the modern road network. Of these the so-called 'Corn Road', linking Hexham to the then port of Alnmouth and the coach road to Edinburgh, which now forms the route of the modern day A697, are fine examples, along which many original features from stone bridges to former coaching inns are still to be seen.

Above left: View from Rothley Castle, an 18th century folly
Above right: Hay Farm, Ford

To export the surpluses of agricultural produce which were being generated in Northumberland, ports were improved and developed. At Berwick-upon-Tweed, Alnmouth and Seahouses extensive new granaries were built to accommodate this trade. The import of vast quantities of bird lime, or guano, from South America for use as fertiliser was a curious consequence of the programme of agricultural

improvement and – at a safe distance from the settlement – the ruins of a large guano shed can still be seen on the estuary of the River Aln. The leading agricultural port, Berwick, was also renowned for its salmon fishery and for the export of salmon in the swift Berwick smacks.

During the 19th century the Northumberland coast supported an important herring fishing industry with harbours such as Holy Island, Seahouses, Craster, Blyth and Newbiggin-by-the-Sea accommodating substantial fishing fleets. In Seahouses alone 6000 barrels of herring were shipped from the port in 1843-44. Today, the upturned hulls of fishing boats alongside Holy Island harbour, now used as storage sheds, provide the sole remaining evidence of this industry. The Northumberland coast has always been treacherous for shipping with the cliffs and reefs of the Farne Islands presenting a particular hazard to mariners and being the cause of numerous shipwrecks. It was the rescue of survivors from the stricken steam ship, the Forfarshire, on the Farne Islands in 1838, which attracted public fascination at the time and propelled the Longstone Lighthouse keeper's daughter, Grace Darling, to national fame.

The 18th and early 19th centuries were also peak years of an ancient agricultural trade, the droving of cattle from Scotland. Throughout the Northumberland uplands hollow ways in the heather and grass still mark the routes where countless

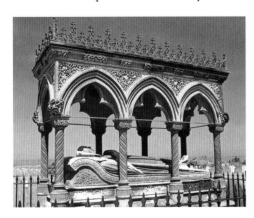

thousands of cattle were driven to market. On land at Stagshaw Bank, near Corbridge, great fairs were once held for cattle which had been herded down the well-trodden route of Dere Street. The cattle market at Morpeth, on the Great North Road, was supposedly the largest outside Smithfield in London.

Top left: Farm worker's cottages near Wooler
Above right: Upturned herring fishing boats, Holy Island
Left: Effigy and shrine of Grace Darling, Bamburgh

With the great wealth generated from their estates, many of the major landowners and industrialists in Northumberland built fine stately homes with gardens and grounds landscaped in the new fashions of the time. In the forefront of this movement was Sir William Lorraine of Kirkharle who, in the early 18th century, was to enhance his estate through building works and most notably by landscape improvements. It is recorded that he planted 24,000 forest trees, 488,000 hedgerow shrubs and 580 fruit trees on his modest estate but of perhaps greater significance still was the fact that he provided an apprenticeship for the young Lancelot 'Capability' Brown. The work of Capability Brown in creating classically ordered parkland landscapes with sweeping 'natural' vistas was to achieve national renown.

Near to Kirkharle on the extensive Wallington estates (now partly in the ownership of the National Trust), building and landscape works of an astonishing scale and complexity were undertaken. In addition to the impressive Hall and surrounding gardens, extensive lakes and a dramatic mock castle and fort were created. These latter features may still be seen at Rothley, some four miles distance from Wallington Hall. Hulne Park at Alnwick, with its spectacular landscape and building designs, including Brizlee Tower and Hulne Priory, was created for the first Duke of Northumberland during this 18th century period with contributions from both Robert Adam and Capability Brown. Developing this landscape tradition in a later period, Lord Armstrong, whose fortune had been made in naval shipbuilding and armaments industries on Tyneside, was to undertake forest tree planting on an extensive scale within his 14,000 acre (5665 hectare) estate at Cragside. The dramatic Cragside House and the surrounding woodlands and lakes (which once powered the first domestic electricity supply) are also now in the ownership of the National Trust.

The desire to create improvement and order in rural Northumberland was to achieve further expression in the creation of model villages. The most picturesque of these are at Blanchland in the south of the County and Ford in the north. A settlement formed within the outer court of the old Norman abbey, the village of Blanchland served the nearby lead mines and was described by John Wesley in 1747 as being "little more than a heap of ruins". By a circuitous route the village was acquired by Lord Crewe, the Bishop of Durham, in the early 18th century and on his death by the Lord Crewe Trustees. Inspired by developing ideas on social reform the Trustees were to direct parts of their estate income into improving conditions within the village, including the reconstruction of houses, the building of a school and the provision of a safe water supply.

Portrait of Lancelot 'Capability' Brown by Nathaniel Dance

In the midst of an estate which was subject to radical agricultural improvements during the second half of the 18th century by the Delaval family, the village of Ford remained typical of the still basic and impoverished small rural settlements of Northumberland until the mid-19th century. Coming to Ford in 1860, Louisa, Marchioness of Waterford remodelled Ford Castle as her residence and then directed her attention to the improvement of the village itself and to the lives of her estate workers. The school building, decorated with her own paintings of biblical scenes, and the smithy with an ornate horseshoe style entrance, are amongst the buildings which show evidence of her endeavours, work that has been continued under the Joicey family as succeeding owners of the estate.

Whilst this period was one of generally increasing wealth and radical change in rural Northumberland, these benefits did not flow to the mass of the labour force, whose lives continued to be ruled by poverty and hardship. Now known mainly for his remarkable engravings of wildlife, the Northumberland artist Thomas Bewick also worked to record the sufferings of the rural poor during this period.

The picturesque settlement of Etal, near Ford, would have been typified by rural squalor during these times. As late as 1882 the 'Berwick Advertiser' reported of Etal, "most females brought up in this village die of consumption and the men of typhoid". Less than a mile from the village of Blanchland, the failure of local lead mines forced families from their homes as the population of the hamlet of Shildon declined from 160 to 40 in the space of two decades. Conditions for workers on the new farms were harsh in the extreme. Until the 20th century, agricultural labourers, known as 'hinds', were only given contracts of employment for one year at a time and were bound themselves to engage a female worker or 'bondager'. According to an inspector's report in the early 19th century these labourers 'make part of the livestock of the farm'. A new rural landscape had been created in Northumberland, but improvements to human lives were not a necessary accompaniment to improvements on the land.

Moving on – until the beginning of the 20th century many agricultural workers were employed on contracts for a single year. May 12th each year was 'flitting day' when workers took to the road with their families and belongings

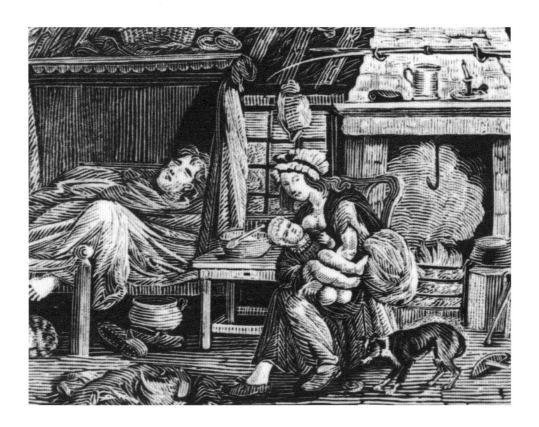

Late 18th century cottage interior, engraving by Thomas Bewick

Granary in Dewars Lane, Berwick-upon-Tweed. During the late 18th and early
19th centuries, Berwick was the pre-eminent agricultural port in
Northumberland and one of the leading grain ports in Britain

Top: The Smithy, Ford
Above: Packing herring, Blyth

Top: Cattle Market, Morpeth
Above: Roadside market, near Alwinton

Top: Agricultural workers and overseer, near Wooler
Above: A brigantine, the 'Peace', unloading timber at Alnmouth

Top: Lime kilns, Holy Island
Above: Shepherd's House, Dod Law

Rothley Castle. A spectacular gothic folly built for Sir Walter Calverley Blackett
to overlook his estate

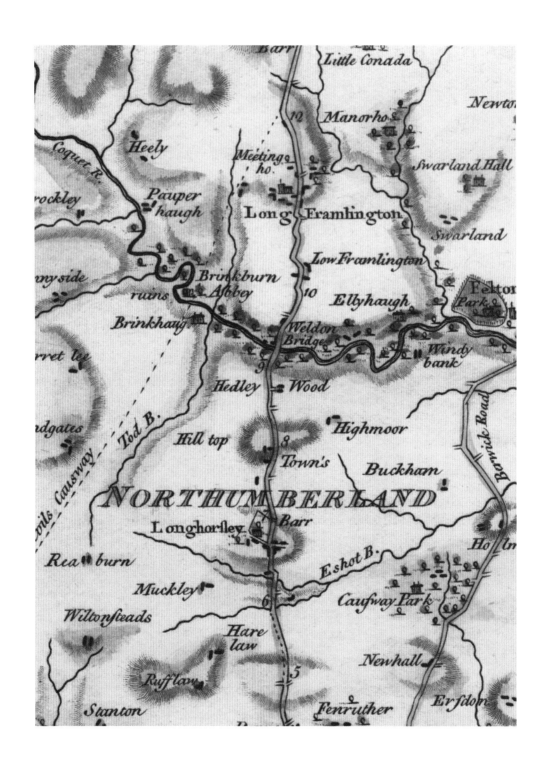

London to Edinburgh coach road
Armstrong 1776

Weldon Bridge and the Anglers Arms. Bridge and inn on the
former coach road to Edinburgh

Hulne Priory. Dating from 1242, this is one of the earliest English foundations
of the Carmelites. The site was the subject of extensive work by
Robert Adam and Capability Brown in the 18th century
as part of the improvement of Hulne Park

Brizlee Tower. Built by the first Duke of Northumberland in 1781,
to a design probably provided by Robert Adam, the Tower is a
spectacular landmark in Hulne Park

Wallington Hall with grotesque dragon's heads. Originally built by
Sir William Blackett in 1688 from his lead and coal mining and shipping fortunes.
The Hall was redesigned by his great-nephew Sir Walter Calverley Blackett
and later by the Trevelyan family

Right: Cragside. The country house of the first Lord Armstrong
and the centre of 14,000 acre (5665 ha) estate

Seaton Delaval Hall. Designed for Admiral George Delaval by Sir John Vanbrugh,
neither were alive to witness the completion of this imposing building in 1729

Cambo. A planned village on the Wallington estate

North Sunderland harbour and Seahouses village. During the 19th and early
20th centuries, herring fishing was a major industry at Seahouses with fish being
exported to ports as far distant as Hamburg, Danzig and St Petersburg.
The limekilns at the top right of the photograph were built in the 1770s
and supplied quick lime to the Scottish market

Etal village. Once common throughout rural Northumberland the thatched cottages
and pub now make Etal distinctive. This picturesque village was largely rebuilt by
Lord Joicey in the early 20th century

Top: Paine's Bridge. An ornamental bridge over the River Wansbeck
on the 'Corn Road'. Overlooked from Wallington Hall,
this elaborate ballustraded bridge was designed by James Paine

Above: Bridge over the River Till. An 18th century bridge
on the former toll road

Blanchland. A village remodelled by the Lord Crewe Trustees in the 18th century
within the grounds of the old abbey

REVOLUTIONS
in STEAM

West Wylam Railway Bridge

The radical changes to the management of land in Northumberland, which transformed the rural landscape, were accompanied by an ever-increasing exploitation of other natural resources. In turn the industries fed by this exploitation created wholly new urban landscapes within the County.

Whilst Northumberland remained essentially a rural county throughout the 18th century, an ever-increasing proportion of the population was turning to industrial work to secure income on which they could survive. An early example of this process of change was to be found in the now peaceful dales of the North Pennines. Here, in scattered mines, lead ore had been won from the ground since early medieval and possibly Roman times. However, during the 18th century, this rather haphazard local industry was transformed as production became dominated by a few major companies and new techniques of working were introduced. The small hamlet of Allenheads in the East Allen valley became the centre for the richest lead mine in Europe at that period. Here, a series of reservoirs in the surrounding hills powered the machinery for mine workings which stretched deep underground and workers undertook every stage of production, from extracting the ore to its final smelting. On the edges of the high moorlands around the village, farmsteads and

smallholdings were established within which families supplemented the poor living gained from the mines. Lead mining continued to be the dominant North Pennines industry until late in the 19th century, when competition from abroad and diminishing reserves brought about its decline and closure. Features of the lead industry still abound in the North Pennine dales and uplands, including the ruins of mines, mill chimneys and flues, former packhorse routes across the moors and the homes, schools and chapels of the mining families.

At the eastern extreme of the County, Seaton Sluice offers a contrasting example of early, major industrial development. Here, the Delaval family developed the 'Royal Northumberland Bottle Works' in 1762 that became the largest glassworks in the country. To serve the glassworks, their nearby coal works and other local industries, the Delavals improved the small natural harbour at Seaton Sluice by cutting a new entrance to the sea through the sandstone cliffs. Completed in 1764, this entrance, the 'New Cut', remains a dramatic feature of the long-abandoned commercial harbour and a testimony to the dynamism of the early industrial entrepreneurs in Northumberland.

Many of the early industries in Northumberland made use of the abundant streams and rivers in the County as their source of power. On the River Till, near Ford, the Heatherslaw Watermill, now open to the public, offers a fine working example of a Northumbrian corn mill which would at one time have been a common feature on watercourses throughout the County.

Former school established for the lead mining community at Carr Shield, West Allendale

Otterburn Mill, on the River Rede, served a long history as a woollen mill and retains many features of a once important local industry. At Guyzance, on the River Coquet, is one of the most spectacular dams of the early industrial period designed by the famous civil engineer, John Smeaton. The mill powered by this dam had a typically chequered history, serving variously as an iron and tin foundry, and a woollen mill. The great reserves of stone of suitable quality for building work were a further natural resource which was exploited throughout the County. The accelerating programmes of road and building construction from the 18th century onwards saw quarries of all scales developed wherever useable stone outcropped in accessible locations. A once common industry in areas with suitable sandstone rock was the production of millstones and grindstones. Amongst the heather in the Fell Sandstone uplands of the County part-carved, abandoned millstones still remain a common sight.

The industry that was to transform the landscape of south and east Northumberland and which was to place the County at the forefront of the industrial revolution was coal. Coal mining in the County has a long history starting in the Roman period and being relatively widespread in medieval times. Records for the ancient woodland which now forms Plessey Woods Country Park show the then owners, the monks of Newminster, being granted the right to mine coal in 1214. It was during the 18th century that the construction of horse drawn waggonways between the mines and the coastal ports was to permit the rich coal seams of south-east Northumberland to be commercially exploited. Some of the earliest waggonways in the country were built in Northumberland. The first was located in the Blyth/Bedlington area and built around 1604. The more famous Plessey Waggonway was constructed towards the end of the 17th century and provided the link between collieries at Plessey Checks and the quayside at Blyth. It was on the Wylam Waggonway in Northumberland that William Hedley was to draw coal with his early steam locomotives, Puffing Billy and Wylam Dilly. An extraordinary centre for developments which would transform the industrial history of the nation, Wylam was also the birthplace of the great railway engineer, George Stephenson, whose cottage is conserved and open to the public. A walk from Wylam along the line of the former Scotswood, Newburn and Wylam Railway (now part of the Tyne Riverside Country Park) provides access to the magnificent West Wylam Railway Bridge. This was the world's first single span wrought iron railway bridge to carry a suspended rail deck and supposedly the inspiration for the Sydney Harbour Bridge. It was Northumberland engineers too who solved the problem of creating iron rails which were of sufficient strength and flexibility to accommodate the massive weight of steam engines. At the famous Bedlington Ironworks, on the banks of the River Blyth, the first high quality malleable iron rails were produced together with many early steam locomotives.

Part completed millstone, Harbottle Hills

127

These engineering achievements provided the basis for the development of a network of railways which were to provide a vital new link between urban and rural Northumberland and exhibit some remarkable examples of industrial architecture.

Opened in 1835, the line between Blaydon and Hexham (later extending to Carlisle) was an early undertaking and the world's first lineside stations were built for the main settlements along this route. The most impressive example of architectural engineering was to be in the north of the County where Robert Stephenson designed the magnificent Royal Border Bridge over the River Tweed at Berwick-upon-Tweed. During a time of fierce competition between the North Eastern and North British railway companies a complex web of rail lines was established in the second half of the 19th century linking towns and industries throughout Northumberland. In remote locations such as Redesmouth, near Bellingham, new communities were established to service the railways and on seemingly modest rural branch lines astonishing structures such as the viaduct near Lambley were constructed. Rising 110 feet (34 m) above the South Tyne this monument to the optimism of the railway age has been recently restored and is accessible to the public. The cheap transport offered by the railways brought about profound changes to the economy of the County and to ways of life. The prosperity

of the main coal mining and industrial areas was enhanced and for settlements such as Allendale Town, Rothbury, Seahouses, Alnmouth and Newbiggin-by-the-Sea the railways brought new income from holidaymakers. Yet the long tradition of cattle droving was brought to an end by this new means of transport and the great droving fairs became only a memory. Likewise, the era of the stagecoach was concluded and for coaching towns such as Belford and for the widespread network of coaching inns, the consequence was hardship.

The railway revolution and the application of steam power for pumping water from the mines enabled a great expansion of coal production to take place in Northumberland during the 19th century. The output of the Northumberland collieries rose from 1,053,274 tons in 1794 to 6,463,550 tons in 1874 and to 9,541,199 tons in 1894. Throughout large parts of Northumberland, the pithead gear and the heaps of numerous collieries became distinctive landscape features, but nowhere were these more concentrated than on the coastal plain from Amble to Newcastle. A massive increase in population occurred in the south-east of the County as workforces were drawn in to support the newly establishing mines and industries. Bedlington, a small rural village with medieval origins, grew rapidly into an industrial settlement in the mid-19th century as mines were sunk. Ashington in the mid-19th century was no more than a single farm. By 1890, however, the Ashington Coal Company had developed 11 rows with a total of 665 houses and over the next quarter of a century a further 1300 houses were added.

Lambley Viaduct

On the coast, small harbours were to become complex industrial ports. Foremost amongst these new ports was Blyth. Following the formation of the Blyth Harbour and Dock Company in 1854 and the later establishment of the Blyth Harbour Commission, it became one of Europe's leading coal ports and a centre for shipbuilding, ship repairing and heavy engineering. Amble, at the mouth of the River Coquet did not exist as a port in the 18th century but by the early 20th century had a coal trade amounting to 750,000 tons per annum.

For the great landowners of the County, such as the Ridleys, the Delavals and the Percys, this period resulted in a remarkable generation of wealth. This was reflected in a programme of country house construction in which the famous Newcastle architect, John Dobson, had a wide influence. Longhirst Hall, Nunnykirk Hall, Matfen Hall and Hartford Hall are amongst the fine buildings of this period. The buildings which served the mine workers were on an altogether more modest scale, with lines of terraced housing, Methodist chapels, co-operative stores and working men's clubs being common elements in many mining settlements. A distinctive culture developed in the mining communities based on shared experience of hardship. The annual Northumberland Miners' Picnic, which was both a political meeting and a family festival, was a highlight of the calendar. The bands and the

banners of the colliery lodges provided the rallying points for miners in both celebration and protest. The mining communities also developed their own recreational and sporting traditions and Northumberland family names such as Milburn and Charlton were in the 20th century to be associated with outstanding achievements in football.

Above left: Ashington, functional terraced housing for coal miners
Above right: Classical elegance, a gazebo in the grounds of Bavington Hall

The remarkable technical progress of the period of industrialisation was achieved at a heavy human cost. Conditions in the mines and in main industries gave scant regard to human health and welfare. It was not until 1831, with the formation of

'Hepburn's Union', the first miners' union for Northumberland and Durham, that strike action was organised which won a limit of 12 hours to the working day for children in the mines. Lack of basic provision of a means of escape for miners underground was to lead to the horrific Hartley Colliery disaster of 1862 when the broken beam of the pumping engine plunged down the mineshaft and sealed the miners underground. The monument in Earsdon churchyard to the 204 men and boys killed in this tragedy is a testimony to the human suffering of the period.

The end of the 19th century and the first years of the 20th century marked the high point of mining and heavy engineering industry in Northumberland. In 1895 Cadwallader J Bates in the last paragraph of his 'History of Northumberland' wrote, "Agriculture has suffered comparatively less in Northumberland than in many other counties: still, the problem of how to keep any population on the land is none the less pressing. It is harrowing to see in many districts the ruins of what until recently were smiling homesteads, where stalwart families were brought up in health and happiness. What will occur in the not distant future, when the coalfields will be exhausted, it is difficult to foresee". It is the consequences of this prophesied collapse in the 19th century industrial base of Northumberland and the progress in creating a new economy and society which are the subject of our final chapter.

Miners pulling coal tub

Memorial to the workmen who lost their lives in the Woodhorn Colliery
explosion on August 13th 1916

Friends' Meeting House, East Coanwood. A typically plain place of worship
for the mining and farming communities in the North Pennines

Right: George Stephenson's Cottage, near Wylam.
Birthplace of the great engineer

Top: Heatherslaw Watermill. Working machinery for flour milling
Above: Heatherslaw Watermill. External view of mill building

Seaton Sluice

Top: Coal miners with pony

Above: Bedlington Ironworks. Little now remains to be seen of this industrial site
by the River Blyth which had a major role in railway development

Top: Old locomotive engine, Wylam. Watercolour painting by
Thomas Hair of steam engine originally built by William Hedley in 1813

Above: Hartley Colliery. Watercolour painting by Thomas Hair of Hartley Colliery
in the mid 19th century. At this time coal was hauled by horses on a waggonway
which linked to staiths in the purpose built harbour at Seaton Sluice

Top: Coal being loaded from the staiths at Blyth. Mainly developed during the 19th century to serve the surrounding mines. Blyth in its heyday shipped more coal than any other port in Europe

Above: Inside George Stephenson's cottage, near Wylam

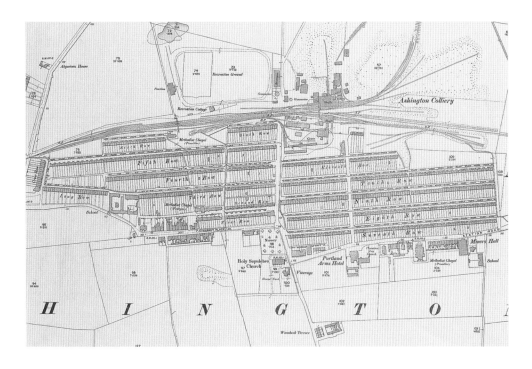

Top: 1897 Ordnance Survey map showing the 11 rows of terraced houses built by
the Ashington Coal Company for their workers

Above: Ashington Football Club. Football was the main sporting interest
in the mining communities

Winding wheel, Woodhorn Colliery Museum. The buildings of the former colliery are one of the few direct links to the great 19th century development of the Northumberland coal mines

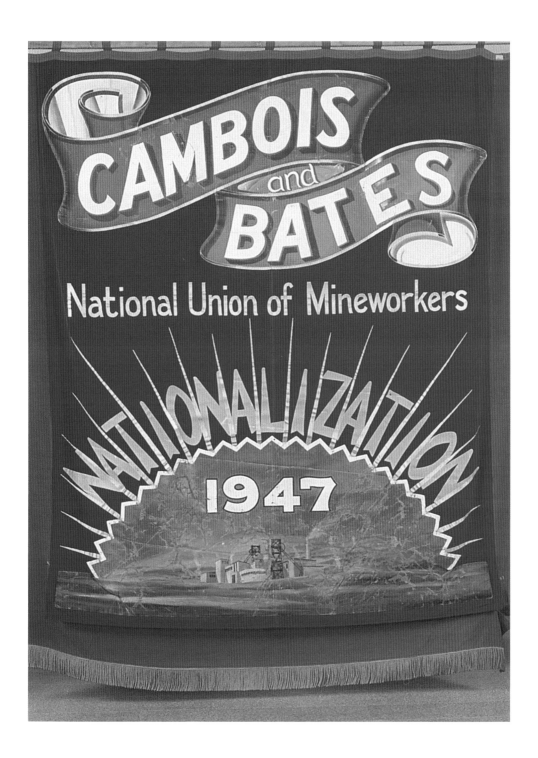

Banner from the Cambois and Bates colliery lodge celebrating the supposed
bright future for the coal mining industry following nationalisation

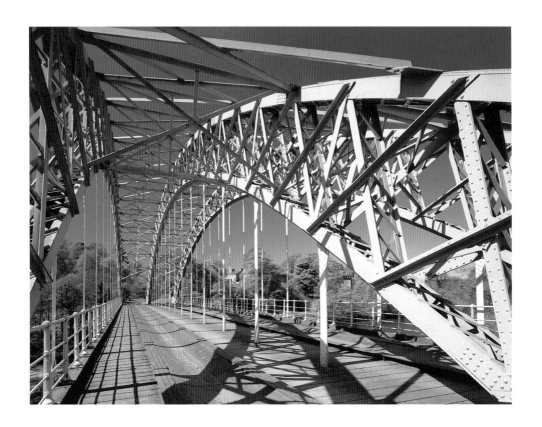

West Wylam Railway Bridge. Designed by William George Laws in 1876,
this bridge continued the remarkable record of engineering
innovation in the Wylam area

Royal Border Bridge. Completed in 1850, this bridge by Robert Stephenson
rises 126ft (38m) above the River Tweed and forms an impressive testimony
to the architecture of the railway age

Top: Picking coal from the tip at Ashington Colliery during the 1911 strike
Above: Loading coal underground. Watercolour painting by Thomas Hair

Matfen Hall

Chimney stack of Shildon engine house, near Blanchland. The ruined engine house
built in 1809 marks an unsuccessful attempt to harness steam power to pump water
from the deep and ancient mine workings at Shildon. These were once an
important source of silver

Chimney of colliery in Haltwhistle Burn

A New Identity

Royal Northumberland Yacht Club, Blyth

The first decades of the 20th century marked a high point for the deep coal mining and heavy industries which had transformed the landscape and economy of significant parts of Northumberland in the preceding 100 years. In 1913 productivity from the coal mines of south-east Northumberland reached a peak, with new pits coming into maximum production to supply a booming market in steam and household coals. The Northumberland and Durham coalfield at that high point was producing an annual total of 56 million tons of coal and employing 25% of all colliery workers in Great Britain. Coal from Northumberland was principally destined for export and the coal ports of Blyth and Amble were busy

and prosperous. In 1913 indeed, the splendid new offices for the Blyth Harbour Commissioners were built. All did appear to be set fair for continuing prosperity.

Elsewhere within Northumberland there were stark reminders of the finite life of all mining industries. In the North Pennines, as has been seen, lead mining, which was once the main source of income for a large proportion of the local population, fell into steep decline

in the face of outside competition and diminishing reserves. Within the space of a few decades towards the end of the 19th century, the industry went from boom conditions to near closure. In Allendale parish the population diminished from 6401 in 1861 to 2763 in 1901 and the legacy of abandoned workings and dwellings is still to be seen.

The decline of the Northumberland coal industry has been more protracted than that of lead mining but, with vastly greater numbers employed, the human cost has been more severe. That decline first became evident in the inter-war years when the depression of the 1930s impacted harshly on the mines and heavy industry in the County and forced many families to leave the area. It was following the Second World War and the nationalisation of the coal industry in 1947, however, that the period of accelerated pit closures began. When the National Coal Board was formed there were 68 working pits in Northumberland, a figure which within two decades was reduced to 21. By the end of a further period of harsh rationalisation, in the 1980s only one substantial deep mine remained in Northumberland. Collieries such as Ashington, which at one stage employed 5000 men and had an output of 1.5 million tons of coal a year, seemed destined to exist only as memories. Both Blyth and Amble were to lose their main function as coal exporting ports and the heavy industries which coal had fed experienced a matching decline. This massive change in the employment base of the most populous part of the County was to result in a legacy of acute problems for both communities and the environment.

Above left: Blyth Harbour Commissioners' Offices
Above right: Abandoned lead miner's cottage, above Allenheads

Rural Northumberland was to face a similarly acute period of change during the 20th century. The demise of the North Pennines lead industry has already been noted and throughout the rural areas generally the closure of mines and major industries was a precursor to problems which would be experienced in the urbanised south-east of the County. Abandoned structures such as Ridsdale Ironworks, near West Woodburn, the several mining and manufacturing works along the Haltwhistle Burn and the chimneys and engine houses of the Stublick and the Ford Moss Collieries, all bear witness to the demise of once important industries. Accompanying this decline was the loss of many of the branch railways which

once probed into the deepest parts of rural Northumberland. Although less dramatic in its physical manifestations than the agricultural revolution of the late 18th and early 19th centuries, the 20th century witnessed massive changes to employment on the land. Mechanisation and changes in land management resulted in a large-scale loss of farm employment. Agricultural workers now occupy few of the rows of purpose-built cottages which were such a characteristic feature of the large Northumberland farm.

The story of Northumberland in the second half of the 20th century and into the 21st century, centres upon attempts to address the consequences of these profound changes and to adapt to and anticipate contemporary demands. Attracting new employment to the south-east of the County, addressing the problems of poor housing and a blighted environment have been major priorities. Beginning in the 1950s, the development of the new town of Cramlington by the County Council showed a new direction for living and working in urban Northumberland which moved from dependency on coal. The construction of new communication routes and industrial infrastructure were essential to this regeneration process, with the development of the A186 Northumberland Spine Road following in the tradition of the major 18th century road building schemes. Within and around the former coal port of Blyth, provision was made for new commerce and industry and within Amble harbour a marina was opened.

Above left: Stublick Colliery, near Hexham
Above right: Ridsdale Ironworks

A massive programme of land reclamation and environmental regeneration was also undertaken, resulting in 1100 hectares of derelict and contaminated land being returned to active use. Launched in 1974, the Ashington Reclamation Scheme was the largest of its kind ever undertaken in Britain, restoring 740 acres (300 ha) of land which contained over 10 million cubic metres of mining waste from the biggest spoil heap in Europe. The generation of new employment opportunities through the establishment of the Wansbeck Business Park has been one element of this scheme. New environments for recreation and nature conservation have been

created from the legacy of deep mining and more recent opencast extraction. Druridge Bay Country Park, the adjoining East Chevington wetland reserve and the Queen Elizabeth II Country Park, near Ashington, are prominent examples of such achievements. The transformation of the landscape of the former coalfield area has resulted in the attraction of firms which place a high value on the quality of the environment. Within south-east Northumberland there is now the greatest concentration of pharmaceutical industries in the north of England and the fastest growing manufacturing industry is that of electronics. The heritage of coal and associated industries is also now becoming of importance to the regeneration of south-east Northumberland. Created only eight years after the closure of the deep mine, Woodhorn Colliery Museum is now an important attraction within the County.

In the rural areas of Northumberland also, developments of comparable scale have transformed the environment and economy during the 20th century. With the future prospects of upland farming appearing uncertain, extensive areas of remote countryside were planted with commercial forests. The peak of this planting programme was to occur between 1945 and 1960 when the vast extent of Kielder Forest finally took shape. The largest area of planted forest in Europe, Kielder and the other major forests in Northumberland have been required to adapt to the radically changing demands on our countryside. Originally planted with the single purpose of timber production, the forests have now been redesigned to enhance the landscape and wildlife interest of the uplands and provide a range of recreational opportunities.

Above left: Restored mining site, East Cramlington
Above right: Cyclists, Wark Forest

152

During the 20th century the sparsely inhabited uplands of Northumberland were seen not only to be a potential timber resource for the nation but also a regional resource for fresh water. Completed in 1905 to supply Newcastle and Gateshead, Catcleugh Reservoir transformed the landscape of the upper valley of the River Rede and provided a foretaste of a more vast engineering feat in the North Tyne Valley. Forming behind a dam which is over 1250 yards (1100 m) long, Kielder Reservoir was completed in 1980 and now extends for over 7 miles (11 km) impounding 44,000 million gallons (200,000 million litres) of water from the North Tyne. As with the surrounding Kielder Forest, the

functional value of Kielder Water has now been matched by its importance for tourism, recreation and conservation. Throughout Northumberland the attention which has been given to improving the quality of river and coastal waters is being reflected in benefits to wildlife. The return of the otter to many Northumberland rivers is one of the most welcome indicators of success.

Continuing a long established tradition, the army retains a considerable presence in Northumberland with the Otterburn Ranges forming one of the most important military ranges in the country. Again, this area of wild landscape is now also being managed to conserve its own special qualities.

Farming is experiencing challenging problems, with employment on the land and on the hill farms in particular continuing to decline. Indications of a more hopeful future are, nevertheless, emerging with the development of closer links between the farming and tourism industries, increasing grant payments for conserving the qualities of the countryside and recognition amongst the public of the quality of Northumberland farm produce.

Improved communication networks have also allowed people to live in and enjoy the environment of Northumberland whilst working outside the County. Within towns such as Hexham, which had regular railway services, housing was developed during the 19th century for people working in Tyneside. By the turn of that century housing for people working in the urban areas was spreading more widely and in the Darras Hall settlement near Ponteland an early attempt was made to establish a garden city. Major improvements to the road network in the 20th century have allowed people to work at considerable distances from their homes and to retire to rural villages which would previously have been seen to be unacceptably isolated. With these developments the decline of many rural villages and market towns has been arrested and new prosperity introduced. The expansion in use of the private car and generally increasing affluence have, in their turn, however, brought new pressures on the environment of the County which have required to be addressed.

Ferry on Kielder Reservoir

Tourism and leisure have grown to be important sources of employment in Northumberland and it is the unspoilt environment and unrivalled heritage of the County which are the principal assets for these industries. Welcoming visitors and investors to Northumberland, whilst at the same time ensuring the qualities they value are not compromised, has become a major challenge. The establishment of the Northumberland National Park in 1956 and the designation of Areas of Outstanding Natural Beauty (AONBs) within the North Northumberland Coast and the North Pennines, have provided mechanisms through which a balance between recreation and conservation can be achieved within some of our finest landscapes. Similar concerns to balance contemporary demands and conservation needs have led to the declaration of sites such as the Farne Islands as National Nature Reserves, Hadrian's Wall as a World Heritage Site and the establishment of the 80 mile length of the Hadrian's Wall National Trail. In new developments, opportunities are increasingly being taken to assimilate modern interests with past heritage and traditions. The creation of The Alnwick Garden, which takes forward the spirit of the great age of landscape gardening in Northumberland, is a remarkable example.

The historic centres of many of Northumberland's towns are being regenerated through investment which aims to enable contemporary use and conservation to be mutually supportive.

In the 21st century Northumberland can be seen to have come of age as a county. With the centuries of wars and lawlessness now deep in history and adjustments having been made to once dislocating forces of social and economic change, Northumberland is entering a period of increased self confidence. There is renewed pride in the County's history, achievements and environment and a desire to ensure its special qualities are safeguarded. New investment is resulting in inherited problems being overcome and is establishing the infrastructure and industries on which a modern period of security and prosperity may be based. A renaissance of artistic and cultural achievement is being experienced throughout the whole of the North East region and is impacting strongly within Northumberland. At the present time consideration is being given to the establishment of regional structures of government. It was Northumberland that was at the centre of the last flowering of a dynamic regional culture fourteen centuries ago. The red and gold flag of the ancient kingdom of Northumbria has been kept alive in this County and with roots established in a long heritage, a vigorous and outward looking future is a realistic aspiration for Northumberland in the 21st century.

Windfarm, Blyth Harbour

Sculpture and town centre improvements, Amble

Fishing coble, Newbiggin-by-the-Sea

Windsurfing, Druridge Bay Country Park

Druridge Bay

Royal Border Bridge, Berwick-upon-Tweed. Night time illuminations

Roman army re-enactment, Hadrian's Wall

Following the Wall. Route of the new Hadrian's Wall National Trail

Top: Alnwick Fair
Above: Judging sheep, Alwinton Show

New landscapes. Kielder Forest and Reservoir

Top: Tumbleton Lake, Cragside
Above: Sheep in a winter landscape, near Bolam

Top: Otter
Above: Red Squirrel

Top: Carlisle Park, Morpeth
Above: Wallington Walled Garden

Cuthbert of Farne by Fenwick Lawson ARCA. Commissioned by the
Northern Rock Foundation

Bolam Lake Country Park, near Belsay

Chillingham Castle gardens

The Alnwick Garden Grand Water Cascade
Right: The Alnwick Garden. Path through pergola of hornbeam

I N D E X

Photographs and Illustrations are indicated in bold print

Æthelburh 50
Æthelfrith 50
Agricola 31, 33
Alexander II 72
Allendale 12, 126, 128, 150
Allenheads 126, 150
Alnmouth 24, 66, 101, 102, 109, 128
Alnmouth cross shaft 51, 52
Alnwick 162
Alnwick Castle 74, 87,
Alnwick Garden 154, 170, 171
Alwinton 108, 162
Amble 128, 129, 150, 155
Amble Marina 151
Anglo-Saxon centre, Yeavering 54
Anglo-Saxon Chronicle 52
Anglo-Saxons 50, 51, 51, 52, 64, 66
Ashington 128, 129, 139, 144, 150, 152
Aydon Castle 74, 97
Bamburgh 12, 50, 51, 102
Bamburgh Castle 17, 74, 85
Battle of Carham 72
Bavington Hall 129
Beadnell 10
Bedlington 72, 127, 128
Bedlington Ironworks 127, 136
Belford 128
Bellingham 128
Belsay Hall and Quarry 21
Bernicia 50
Berwick-upon-Tweed 73, 74, 102, 106, 128
Berwick Barracks 77, 77
Berwick Bridges 77, 128, 143, 159
Berwick Walls 75, 88, 92
Bishop of Durham 72
Black Middens Bastle 77
Blanchland 73, 82, 103, 104, 123
Blyth 102, 107, 127, 129, 138, 149, 150, 151, 154
Blyth Harbour Commissioners Offices 150, 150
Bolam Lake Country Park 168
Bonnie Prince Charlie 77, 101
Breamish Valley 33, 41
Brinkburn Priory 73, 81
Brizlee Tower 103, 115
Bronze Age 30, 30, 31, 31, 34, 39, 47
Brough Law 31, 41
Budle Bay 30
Cadwalla 50
Cadwallader J Bates 130
Cambo 119
Capability Brown 103, 103
Carboniferous period 10, 11, 24
Carr Shield 126
Catcleugh Reservoir 153
Cawfields 32
Chesters 33, 42
Cheviot Hills 10, 11, 13, 18, 19, 25, 30, 31, 33, 50
Chew Green 31, 33, 46
Chillingham Castle 74, 78, 169
Chillingham Park 31, 73, 78
Chillingham Ridge 12

Coal industry 11, 12, 22, 127, 128, 130, 130, 136, 144, 150
Colliery banners 141
Coquetdale 9
Corbridge 31, 33, 43, 102
Corbridge vicar's pele 74, 94
Corn Road 101
Cragside 103, 117, 164
Cramlington 151, 152
Craster 30, 102
Culley brothers 100
Darras Hall 153
Deira 50
Delaval family 104, 126, 129
Dere Street 31, 33, 102
Devil's Causeway 31
Dod Law 110
Doddington Moors 12, 30
Dorothy Forster 77
Druridge Bay Country Park 30, 151, 152, 157, 158
Duddo Stone Circle 37
Dunstanburgh Castle 12, 26, 74
Eadbald 50
Earl Robert of Northumbria 72
Earsdon churchyard 130
Edlingham Castle 74, 97
Edward I 73
Edward II 74
Edward III 74
Eglingham 31
Elizabeth I 75
Elsdon Tower 74, 74
Etal 104, 121
Etal Castle 75
Farne Islands 12, 27, 52, 65, 102, 154
Fell sandstone 11, 12, 14, 15, 19, 20, 30, 127
Flodden 75, 76, 93
Ford Castle 74, 75, 104
Ford Moss 151
Ford smithy 104, 107
Ford vicar's pele 74
Ford village 30, 101, 103, 104, 126
Friends' Meeting House, East Coanwood 132
'Geordie' Burn 76
George Stephenson 127, 133, 138
Golden Age 51, 52
Grace Darling 102, 102
Hadrian's Wall 12, 16, 31, 32, 32, 33, 44, 45, 50, 101, 154, 160, 161
Halidon Hill 74
Haltwhistle Burn 147, 151
Harbottle Castle 74, 75
Harbottle Hills 12, 15, 127
Hartford Hall 129
Hartley Colliery 130, 137
Heatherslaw Watermill 126, 134
Heavenfield 50, 55
Hen Hole 10, 25
Henry III 72
Hepburn's Union 130
Hexham 50, 52, 101, 128, 153
Hexham Abbey 62, 63, 80

172

Hexham Gaol	76, 76
High Rochester	31
'Hinds' and 'bondagers'	104
Holy Island	51, 53, 57, 67, 69, 72, 73, 74, 96, 102, 102, 110
Horace St Paul	100
Housesteads	33
Howick	30
Hulne Park	73, 103, 114, 115
Humbleton Hill	74
Ice Age	12
Iron Age	10, 31
James I	77, 100
James IV	75
John Smeaton	127
John Wesley	103
Kielder Forest and Reservoir	77, 152, 153, 153, 163
Kirkharle	103
Kyloe Hills	12
Lady's Well, Holystone	73, 83
Lambley viaduct	128, 128
Lime kilns	100, 101, 110, 120
Lindisfarne	12, 51, 52, 96
Lindisfarne Gospels	49, 51, 58, 59
Lindisfarne gravemarker	52, 68
Lindisfarne Priory	73, 79, 167
London to Edinburgh coach road (A697)	101, 112, 113
Longhirst Hall	129
Lord Crewe Trustees	103
Lordenshaws	30, 34, 38
Louisa, Marchioness of Waterford	104
Matfen Hall	129, 145
Mesolithic	30, 30
Milfield Plain	30
Mitford Castle	74, 75
Morpeth	102, 108, 166
Morpeth Castle	74
Museum of Antiquities, Newcastle upon Tyne	52
National Coal Board	150
Neolithic	30
Neville's Cross	74
Newbiggin	30
Newbiggin-by-the-Sea	102, 128, 156
Norham	72, 74
Norham Castle	73, 74, 75, 89
North Pennines	12, 20, 126, 150, 151, 154
Northumberland Coast	154
Northumberland Miner's Picnic	129
Northumberland National Park	33, 154
Nunnykirk	129
Nunnykirk cross shaft	52
Odo of Bayeux	72
Ogle Castle	74
Old Bewick	31
Oswald	50, 51, 52
Oswiu	50
Otterburn	74
Otterburn Mill	127
Otterburn Ranges	153
Paine's Bridge	122
Paulinus	50
Plessey Waggonway	127
Plessey Woods Country Park	127
Poind and his Man, Bolam	35
Ponteland	74, 153
Preston Tower	86
Prudhoe Castle	74, 95
Puffing Billy	127
QE II Country Park	152
Redesdale	76, 100
Redesmouth	128
Reivers	76
Ridsdale Ironworks	151, 151
Robert Adam	103
Robert Stephenson	128
Robert the Bruce	74
Ros Castle	31
Rothbury	30, 52, 128
Rothbury cross shaft	52
Rothley	101, 103, 111
Rothley Crags	11
Roughting Linn	29, 30, 36
Royal Northumberland Bottle Works	126
St Aidan	51, 53, 56
St Aidan, Thockrington	73, 73
St Andrew, Corbridge	73
St Cuthbert	51, 167
St Cuthbert – pendant cross	61
St Cuthbert's Cave	52, 65
St Cuthbert, Inner Farne	65
St Cuthbert Cross	61
St Cuthbert's Island	51, 60
St John the Baptist, Edlingham	73, 73
St Laurence, Warkworth	73, 84
St Wilfrid	52
Seahouses	102, 120, 128
Seaton Delaval Hall	118
Seaton Sluice	126, 135
Shaftoe Crags	11, 20
Shildon	104, 146
Simonside Hills	11, 12, 19
Sir William Lorraine	103
Stagshaw Bank	102
Stanegate	31, 32, 45
Stublick colliery	151, 151
Synod of Whitby	52
The Bizzle	10
Thomas Bewick	100, 104, 105
Threshing machines	101
Tosson Tower	72
Turnpike trusts	101
Tyne Riverside Country Park	127
Union of the Crowns	77, 100
Vikings	52, 72
Vindolanda	31, 33, 45
Wallington Hall	99, 103, 116, 122, 166
Wansbeck Business Park	152
Wark Forest	152
Wark-on-Tweed Castle	74, 75, 90
Wark-on-Tyne Castle	74
Warkworth	71, 74, 91
Weldon Bridge	113
West Wylam Railway Bridge	125, 127, 142
Whin Sill	11, 12, 12, 16, 17, 26, 27
William II	72
William the Conqueror	72
William the Lion	74
Woodhorn Colliery Museum	131, 140, 152,
Woodhouses Bastle	76, 77
Wooler	102, 109
Wylam	127, 137
Wylam Dilly	127
Yeavering	50
Yeavering Bell	31, 40

N Pevsner, I Richmond et al,
*The Buildings of England,
Northumberland,*
Penguin Books, 2nd Edit 1992

C Hardie, S Rushton,
*The Tides of Time: Archaeology on
the Northumberland Coast,*
Northumberland County
Council, 2000

S Beckensall,
Prehistoric Northumberland,
Tempus Publishing Ltd, 2003

G N Wright,
The Northumbrian Uplands,
David and Charles, 1989

M Saler,
*The Old Parish Churches of
Northumberland,*
Fully Publications, 1997

R Newton,
The Northumberland Landscape,
Hodder and Stoughton, 1972

C J Bates,
History of Northumberland,
Sandhill Press, republished, 1996

N Higham,
The Northern Counties to AD1000,
Longman, 1986

J Hawkes,
The Golden Age of Northumbria,
Sandhill Press/Tyne and Wear
Museums, 1996

D O' Sullivan, R Young,
Lindisfarne, Holy Island,
B T Batsford/English Heritage, 1995

J Marsden,
*The Fury of the Northmen, Saints,
Shrines and Sea-Raiders in the
Viking Age,*
Kyle Cathie, 1996

R Lomas,
*County of Conflict, Northumberland
from Conquest to Civil War,*
Tuckwell Press, 1996

G MacDonald Fraser,
The Steel Bonnets,
Harper Collins, 1995

I Macluur,
*A Fortified Frontier, Defences of the
Anglo-Scottish Border,*
Tempus Publishing, 2001

R Fynes,
*The Miners of Northumberland
and Durham,*
Davis Books, republished, 1986

H Edwards,
Follow the Banner,
Carcanet Press, 1997

F Atkinson,
*Life and Tradition in Northumberland
and Durham,*
Smith Seltle, republished, 2001

C J Hunt,
*The Lead Miners of the Northern
Pennines,*
Manchester University Press, 1970

A Raistrick and B Jennings,
*A History of Lead Mining in the North
Pennines,* Longmans, 1965

L Turnbull,
*The History of Lead Mining in the
North East of England,*
Sandhill Press, 1985

J T Tuck,
*The Colleries of Northumberland,
Volumes 1 and 2,*
Trade Union Printing Services, 1993

D Glendinning,
*The Art of Mining, Thomas Hair's
Watercolours of the Great Northern
Coalfield, City of Newcastle upon Tyne,*
Tyne Bridge Publishing, 2000

APPRECIATION

Thanks are due to all who assisted in the preparation of this book.

In particular appreciation is expressed to Dr Stafford Linsley for historical advice and to Brian Young, British Geological Survey, for advice on the first origins of Northumberland.

Amongst these who assisted in the development of the book, special mention is due to Graeme Peacock, Tom Cadwallender, Steve Newman, Alan Cutter, Keith Gilroy, Caroline Hardie, Kevin Patrick, Shirley Cross, Stacy Hall and Rachel Stevinson.

Invaluable work on proof reading was contributed by Margaret Keyte and Liz Williams and for work on typing and retyping the text, special thanks are due to Monica Wright and Madeleine Massey. Appreciation for assistance in collating material is expressed to Helen Hawes and to Barrie Watson of NB GROUP for all design work.

IMAGE ACKNOWLEDGEMENTS

We are grateful to the following individuals and organisations for the loan of photographs and illustrations. All material remains the copyright of the listed contributors. Photographs are by Graeme Peacock (www.graeme-peacock.com) with the exception of

Air Fotos Ltd - p.40, 57

British Geological Survey - p.10, 12, 22

British Library, Picture Library - p.49, 58, 59

C Crossley - p.11, 15, 41, 73, 74, 75, 76, 78, 83, 100, 101, 102, 113, 122, 126, 127, 132, 134, 150

English Heritage Photographic Library (artist P Dunn) - p.54

English Heritage Photographic Library - p.68

English Heritage, National Monuments Record (photographer T Gates) - p.46

Laurie Campbell - p.165

Museum of Antiquities of the University and Society of Antiquaries of Newcastle upon Tyne - p.30, 31, 32, 33, 37, 39, 51, 61

National Portrait Gallery, London - p.103

National Trust - p.100

Newcastle City Council - City Library - p.105

Northumberland County Council - p.65, 73, 90, 97, 146

Northumberland County Record Office - p.104, 106, 107, 108, 109, 129, 136, 138, 139, 150

Northumberland National Park - p.47

Ordnance Survey - p.139

P Crossley - p.77

P Neal - p.112

R J L Smith of Much Wenlock - p.62, 63

S Newman - p.27, 86, 162, 169

S Weightman - p.102

The Chapter Library, The College, Durham - p.61

The Hatton Gallery, University of Newcastle upon Tyne - p.137, 144

Woodhorn Colliery Museum - p.130, 136, 141, 144